THE
MASTER
HAS
COME

SEVEN SERMONS AND OBJECT LESSONS FOR LENT AND EASTER DAY

THOMAS A. PILGRIM

C.S.S. Publishing Co.
Lima, Ohio

THE MASTER HAS COME

Copyright © 1989 by
The C.S.S. Publishing Company, Inc.
Lima, Ohio

LIBRARY OF CONGRESS
Cataloging-in-Publication Data

Pilgrim, Thomas A., 1944-
   The master has come : seven sermons and object lessons for Lent and Easter Day / Thomas A. Pilgrim.
     p.   cm.
  ISBN 1-556-73102-7
  1. Lenten sermons. 2. Easter — Sermons. 3. Sermons, American.
4. Children's sermons. I. Title.
BV4277.P55   1989   88-28305
252'.62—dc19   CIP

9813 / ISBN 1-55673-102-7   PRINTED IN U.S.A.

Table of Contents

*Dedicated
to my wife Shirley who has
supported me in all things
and has helped me learn the
way of the Master*

Foreword

Thomas A. Pilgrim, A Christ-centered minister, has written a Christ-centered book. Captivated by Jesus, this winsome preacher retells the Gospel story of the Master who continually comes into our world and into our lives. Jesus meets us at the point of our need. Through faith he provides us with the spiritual resources to live in newness of life.

An invitational preacher, the author invites the reader to join him on a journey with Christ. Using as his theme "The Master Has Come," he puts the reader in touch with the exciting message and encounters of Jesus' first coming. With his scholarly and imaginative mind he gives a fresh interpretation of the New Testament stories. They become stories to be lived by us in the modern world.

A pastor at heart, the author understands the concern and stresses of Christians. It is his aim to help persons get in touch with resources that will enable them to live a victorious life. He does this by showing the way Christian truth is to be used in our everyday human existence. With a refreshing sense of humor, the author's style of writing is fascinating and inspiring. Drawing upon his own rich pastoral experience and his personal life story, the author makes the Gospel story more real. The Master who has come gives us mastery over our lives.

— Gordon Thompson
Shatford Professor of Homiletics, Retired
Candler School of Theology
Emory University

Preface

There is no other person like Jesus of Nazareth. Of all the men and women who have walked across the pages of history, no other has ever had the impact of his life. From the beginning it was evident that his life had a quality like no other. Everywhere he went men, women, and children felt the impact of his life. They were led to say, "He is the Son of God."

Into the lives of a great many people there came a new calm, a new hope, a new challenge, a new way, a new sense of peace. Into one home in particular a new hope was born because of the words, "The master has come."

That new sense of hope took on an even greater meaning with the Resurrection, and his followers took the Good News to the ends of the earth.

Wherever that story has been told, the lives of people have been made better. The Master has come into every part of the world — into every culture, into every system, and into every walk of life. The affect is ever and always the same.

It is for that reason that I offer the retelling of a part of the story of the Master. The chapters in this book were first shared with the people of my congregation on the Sundays during Lent and Easter. My intent was to look at some of the significant points in the ministry of Jesus, and to see how these great truths still touch us today.

It is my hope and prayer that those who read these words will know in their hearts that the Master has come.

— Thomas A. Pilgrim

Chapter One

Children's Object Lesson

"The Time is Right"

Object: *A Watch*

Good morning boys and girls. I am so glad all of you have come to church today. Does anyone know what today is? It is the first [Sunday/week] in the season of Lent.

"Lent" is a period of forty days, leading up to Easter. It is an important time of the year in the church. During this season we are getting ready for Easter. During the season of Lent I am going to be talking with you about some of the important things which happened during the life of Jesus.

Now, I want to show you my watch today. All of you can see it, can't you? Who can tell us the right time? That is right, it's 11:15, isn't it?

It's really important that we always know the right time. You have to be in school at a certain time. You get out of school at a certain time. You probably have supper each night at a certain time. Your parents want you to go to bed at a certain time. Isn't this true for most of you? We know this is important.

When Jesus first began his ministry, he said, "The time is right." He wanted people to know he had come into the world at just the right time. So, as he began preaching he said to all the people who were listening to him, "The time is fulfilled, and the kingdom of God is at hand; repent, and believe in the gospel."

So, Jesus was saying that it was now time for people to get ready for what God was going to do in the world. God's Kingdom was coming into the world because Jesus was bringing it.

He was beginning a new age when God would be the king of the people's lives. God would rule in their hearts.

And, do you know what, boys and girls? The time is just right for us to let God be our king, the one who rules in our hearts and in our lives. Wouldn't you like for God to be the king of your life? Right now, at your age, the time is right for that to happen.

Prayer: Now, would you bow your hearts? *O God, help us to open our lives to your love and presence, and make you the king of our lives, in Jesus' name. Amen*

Thank you for being here today.

Chapter One

The Master Has Come —
To Proclaim God's Kingdom

Mark 1:9-15

In the novel *Barabbas* there is a scene where a woman who lives with the outcasts in the valley of Ge-Hinnom, outside the gates of the city of Jerusalem, waits for sleep at night. She hears the groanings of the sick. She thinks about Jesus and the kingdom he is always talking about. She thinks the next day will bring an end to suffering.

Later on in the story, after the death of Jesus, many of his followers are persecuted. This woman is led out to the place where people are put to death. A yelling crowd surrounds her, and begins stoning her.

She stretches out her hands and says, "He has come! He has come! I see him!" Then, she falls to her knees and says, "Lord, how can I witness for thee? Forgive me . . ." And, she dies.

There is a phrase in the Gospel of John which, in my mind, sums up the message of the New Testament: "The Master has come." It is a phrase which has intrigued me — captured my imagination — for in that phrase is the answer for which we are all looking. Whatever the problem — the question, the situation, the pain, the sorrow, "the Master has come."

The Master has come, and nothing will ever be the same again. An entirely new element has come into the history of the world. A new song has passed across the lips of men, women, and children. A new note of joy has been sounded. A new source of hope has melted the ice of despair. A new light of victory has streaked across the horizon. A new dawn has broken into a new day. *The Master has come.*

It happened that Jesus came down from Nazareth to the Jordan River where cousin John, the baptizer, was preaching. And, along with many other people Jesus was baptized there. Then the spirit of God descended upon Jesus, and he heard a voice from heaven saying, "Thou art my beloved son; with thee I am well pleased."

Jesus went to the wilderness for forty days — a time of retreat, thought, prayer, strategizing, and testing — being tempted of the devil. Then, Jesus came into Galilee preaching. God had one son, and he made a preacher out of him.

But, why did Jesus preach? Why didn't he write a book, organize an army, run for public office, issue decrees, write letters to the editor, or send petitions to Rome?

The answer is that he came to be the proclaimer — the bearer, the teller, the talker, the preacher, teacher, actualizer of God's kingdom. He came to tell people what God was doing, was about to do, *would* do in the present and future. "The time is fulfilled, and the kingdom of God is at hand; repent, and believe in the gospel." (Mark 1:9-15)

He came to be a preacher, a teacher, a proclaimer. He did not come to be a leader, an organizer, a general, a doctor — a doer of wonders, a miracle worker, a performer of signs and magic, personality, a celebrity. He came to proclaim God's kingdom.

The theme of his preaching and teaching was the Kingdom of God. Miss that, and you do not understand anything about Jesus.

In the Gospel of Mark, at the beginning of Jesus' proclaiming the Kingdom of God, we catch the sense of urgency about this message of his. There needs to be the same urgency about us as we think about what the coming of the Master means today.

I

Three things we must do.

First, we must recognize the urgent moment he produced.

Mark records the message of Jesus as beginning with this statement: "The time is fulfilled." *The time* refers to that urgent moment toward which the prophets had looked — that historic moment when God would break into the history of the world.

Jesus knew that in leaving the carpenter's shop in Nazareth and going down to the Jordan River he was bringing about some magnificent moment. The hour had struck. It was time to begin. He produced an urgent moment.

So today, because the Master has come, we must recognize the urgent moment he produced. But, for many of us these days there is no sense of urgency about our religion, or God, or the church.

Our urgent moments are produced by other things we see as being more important, — "urgent matters." Some of us have a sense of urgency all right, but our sense of urgency is caused by the way we live and not the things we should be living *for*; by our priorities and not the things which should be priorities; by things which cause stress, and not the things we should be stressing.

I read about a lady who suddenly decided she just had to have some rat poison that very day. Her husband was in town and she knew he would drop by the drug store. So, she called and said, "Please give my husband rat poison when he comes in for a coke."

There is a sense of urgency about life for many of us these days.

A man went to see the doctor. He said, "My work absorbs me. I can't sleep at night. I'm living on the ragged edge of my nerves." The doctor told him he needed to learn to relax. He said, "Go to the circus. See the great Grimaldi. Laugh. Have fun. You will be a new man." And the man replied, "But Doc, I *am* the great Grimaldi."

Many people are wondering what is wrong with their lives. They are living in shallows and miseries. They have forgotten that Jesus said, "The time is fulfilled." He has produced an urgent moment which puts everything else in the right perspective.

II

There is a second thing we must do. We must realize the urgent announcement he proclaimed.

Jesus said something about what this urgent moment meant when he said, "The kingdom of God is at hand."

Jesus was bringing in a new age, something entirely different, the new age of God's Kingdom breaking into history from the outside. It made everything new and different from that moment on.

This was the urgent announcement he proclaimed — that the Kingdom of God was at hand, on the way, about to happen, already beginning, not yet here, completely here, and still coming out there in the future.

The Kingdom of God is the rule of God in the lives of people, in the life of the world, to the far corners of the universe.

Jesus used many parables to teach what the Kingdom of God is like. He said the Kingdom of God is like a man who will sell all he has in order to purchase a pearl of great price. He said it is like a seed growing secretly. No one knows it is there, but it grows up and becomes something which bears much fruit. He said it is like a grain of mustard seed. It is the smallest of all seed, but becomes the greatest of all shrubs.

The Kingdom of God is a kingdom within us — all around us, in the world and beyond the world — which knows no boundaries, which offers freedom, which has moral and ethical implications, which is a force for right living, and which calls us not only to be citizens, but also to be ambassadors of the Kingdom.

But it is easy for us to let our citizenship in this kingdom get pushed down toward the bottom of a long list of priorities. We lose sight of it. We turn away from it.

One writer, who grew up in England, tells how as a boy he was walking around his parents' estate one day. One of the tenants' little girls saw him coming. As he walked past her, she held out some flowers. He turned snobbishly away from her, and left her in tears. He said, "That was the first time I ever rejected the Kingdom of God."

How easy for us to do that. When we do, life gets out of kilter. It is not right. Something is wrong, and we know it.

A man was looking through his checkbook. He saw these entries his wife had made: "Beauty shop — $12.50; grocery store — $55.85; gas station — $10.00; E.S.P. — $24.65." He asked, "What is E.S.P.?" She replied, "Error some place."

Something is wrong and we know it. There is an error some place. Yet, the Christian life is a call to make the Kingdom of God a reality in our lives.

Gerald Mann, a Baptist minister in Texas, wrote a book called *Why Does Jesus Make Me Nervous?* He told of going to see his friend Carlyle Marney, and telling him he was thinking of leaving the ministry. When asked why, Mann replied that he was unhappy. Marney said, "Well, you *ought* to quit! Whoever told you that you had a right to be happy? The ministry is no place for the pursuit of happiness . . . it's a place for the pursuit of the Kingdom of God!"

Too many Christians are worshiping the gods of happiness. The Christian life is a call to pursue the Kingdom of God, and to realize it in our living.

III

A third thing we must do is respond to the urgent Gospel Jesus preached.

Jesus also said, "Repent, and believe in the Gospel."

To "repent" means to turn around, to turn toward God, to travel in another direction, to get a new mind.

"Gospel" means good news. It is not "repent and flee the judgment," as John the Baptizer had said, but, "Turn around, get a new mind, and believe the Good News about the Kingdom of God." It is a message which calls for a response. We either reject it or accept it. There is no neutral ground. We cannot say, "I'll wait and see . . . maybe sometime . . . let's weigh our options." There is no option. We must respond *now*. It is *urgent*!

Would we let God's Kingdom be Good News for us? Some times it is *bad* news for us, because we do not really want it. We say we believe in it, but we vote against it. We say we are for it, but only as long as it does not interfere with some special interest close to our hearts, or our pocketbooks. We say we want it, but we mostly reject it.

Though we try to ignore him, and dress him up in our clothing, and put our words in his mouth, and interpret his message according to what we want to hear, Jesus Christ still stands among us and says, "Repent, and believe in the Gospel."

Gospel? Good news about *what*? Good news about God's Kingdom, which calls us away from special-interest and economic considerations, and what is popular, and what the Joneses are doing, and what the neighbors will think, and how I can get ahead, and what diversion I can throw my money into. We are called away from all that superficial fluff, and into the Kingdom of God.

How will you respond to this? You are the only one who knows.

In one of his books, E. Stanley Jones told of being in Russia in 1934. He saw the communists building a new civilization without God, and he said he was shaken by it. But, one day he read those words in Hebrews: "Let us be grateful for receiving a kingdom that cannot be shaken." He lived off those words the rest of that day, the promise of an unshakable kingdom.

The next day he read on a little further, and he came across these words: "Jesus Christ, the same yesterday, today, and forever." He wrote, "In a world of flux and change is there one unchanging person, and is that one unchanging person Jesus Christ? And the answer came back, yes — an unhesitating full-throated, yes. Jesus Christ is not changing." So, he discovered two absolutes — an unshakable kindom, and an unchanging person.

You can make that urgent discovery, for *the Master has come* — to proclaim God's Kingdom.

Chapter Two

Children's Object Lesson

"Follow the Leader"

Object: *A Mirror*

Good morning, boys and girls. I'm glad all of you have come to church today. It's good to see you here this morning.

Now, listen to this. When I was your age, we used to play a game called "follow the leader." I don't know if kids still play this game or not. We would go outside, and one person would be the leader. Everyone else would do what the leader did. If the leader walked on one foot, everyone else walked on one foot. If the leader made a face, everyone else made a face. If the leader rolled on the ground, jumped across the creek, or stood on his head, everyone else did the same thing. It was a funny kind of game.

One of the first things Jesus did was to call some people to be his disciples. Who knows what the word "disciple" means? A disciple is a student. A disciple is a person who learns. The disciples of Jesus were learning how to be like him.

Now, look at this mirror. One way to say what I am talking about is to say Jesus wanted them to "mirror his reflection." He wanted them to look like him, and to have his love in their hearts.

That is what Jesus wants us to do today also.

I want to show you a picture of a modern-day disciple — a person who can be just like Jesus, and reflect his love to other people. Look at this mirror, each one of you. Do you see that person? It is *you,* isn't it?

Isn't that a beautiful person in that mirror? That person you are looking at is a child of God. You are made in God's image, to be like him, and to look like him.

That is what Jesus wants you to do — to be a disciple, to be a person who loves the way God loves, and who learns the way of Jesus.

Prayer: Let's ask God to help us do that. **O God, help us to be disciples, so that other people can see Jesus and your love relected in us. In Jesus' name we pray. Amen**

Thanks for being here today.

Chapter Two

The Master Has Come —
And Calls Disciples

Mark 1:16-20

The Roman legions crossed the English Channel, and landed their small ships at the foot of the cliffs of Dover. The Britons looked down and saw them. They laughed, thinking these Romans could pose no real threat to them. But, the Roman commander ordered his soldiers to burn their boats. There would be no turning back. They were there to stay. They had left their boats for good.

When I read that, it brought to mind that scene early in the Gospel of Mark where Jesus is walking along the beach. Little waves from the Sea of Galilee slip up on the sand.

Jesus looks down the beach as far as he can, and he sees — there in the distance — some fishermen. It is Simon and his brother Andrew. As he draws closer to them, he hears the loud swearing of Simon, and as he walks past where they are, he says to them, "Follow me, and I will make you become fishers of men."

It is strange, the effect those words had upon them. Maybe they knew who this man was. Perhaps they were there at the Jordan, and had seen John baptize him. Perhaps they said, "Why it's Jesus of Nazareth, the one John was talking about. He's calling us to be disciples. Let's go with him."

Mark writes, "Immediately they left their nets and followed him." The three of them went a little further down the beach, and there they found James and John. Jesus called them to be disciples, and they left their father, and the servants in the boat, and went with him. (Mark 1:16-20)

The Master has come — and calls disciples.

We are struck by the fact that among the first things Jesus

did was to gather around himself a group of disciples. While he was in the wilderness praying, thinking, planning, strategizing, he apparently decided that his method would include training intensely a small group who would carry on the work he was beginning. He came out of that time of seclusion, and announced the theme of his campaign: "The time is fulfilled, and the Kingdom of God is at hand; repent, and believe the Gospel."

Then, he chose twelve to be disciples. "Follow me," he said, "and I will make you become fishers of men."

He called them away from fishing for fish, to fishing for *people*. He called them away from fishing nets, to open hands. He called them away from the sea, to an ocean of hurting people drowning on dry land. It was as though he told them to burn their boats there on the beach — for they would never be fishing for fish again. Now, they would be fishing for people.

But, why did Jesus call disciples? Would it have been better not to trust these fishermen with something so important? Why not go to all the major cities — Jerusalem, Athens, Rome — and hold great crusades? Instead, we find Jesus keeping to the back roads, going around to little towns few had ever even heard of — Capernaum, Nazareth, Bethsaida, Bethany.

Side roads, villages, small towns; little people no one knew, who were not important, who did not matter, who had no power, pull, or influence — this is where Jesus spent his time, and in the company of the twelve. During those three years he trained the twelve to become the church. He was the teacher, and they were his students.

So, this is one of the most important episodes in the ministry of Jesus. The Master has come — and calls disciples.

And, the Master is calling *us* — calling *you* and *me* — to be his disciples today. But, what does it mean to follow Jesus? We try to make it sound complicated sometimes. But, it is really pretty simple. No one could say in a few words what it means to follow Jesus. But we can state it fairly simply.

I

First, we find a friend — one whose friendship never ends.
That is the first thing to remember. This is what makes Christian faith different from all other religion.

Bishop Westcott said, "A Christian is essentially one who throws himself with absolute trust upon a living Lord, and not one who endeavors to obey the commands and follow the example of a dead teacher." All the other religions have as their leader a dead teacher. Christian faith has a living Lord.

I love to read theology. I value greatly the historic creeds of the church. Correct belief is vital. We need to know what we believe. But, more importantly, Christian faith is a relationship.

After John Dean, one of the Watergate conspirators, left Washington, and went back to California, he went down to the library and applied for a library card. He had to give a personal reference. The lady at the desk said, "Just put down the name of a friend." He said, "I don't even *have* a friend. If I ever get one I'll come back."

We all need a friend. Jesus chose the twelve to be his friends. Who were they? Nobody. What qualifications did they have? None. How much training, influence, expertise, did they possess? Zero. But, he said to them, "Follow me." He took them on to be disciples. And, later on, he said to them, "No longer do I call you servants. Now I call you my friends."

He took a bowl of water and a towel and got down on his knees in front of them, and washed their feet. He said, "My body I give, and my blood I shed for you."

He promised them they would have the fellowship, the companionship, the friendship of his spirit to guide them, comfort them, strengthen them — always.

You want to know what it means to follow Jesus? It means we find a friend — one whose friendship never ends.

Do you have any idea how far-reaching the implications of that statement are? If Jesus is like God, and God is like Jesus, and Jesus is a friend — *then we live in a friendly universe!* It is not evil. It is not senseless. It is not drifting. It is not purposeless. It is not spinning out of control. The one who is in charge is our friend. We have friends in high places. We have some pull. We have an open line. Someone has given us a season pass.

But, many people do not believe this.

A preacher once told me that a woman phoned him and said, "Are you still praying for me?" When he answered "Yes," she replied, "Well, why isn't it working?" She felt all alone.

Many people in modern society live closed-up lives, behind closed-up doors in closed-up subdivisions. They have closed-up minds, closed-up hearts, closed-up hands. They wall themselves off from people, and from God, and wonder why God is not real to them. But we all have this great need inside to find a friend.

After the battle of Dunkirk, a general landed with his men at a British port. An officer told the general how his men could find the rest center, and offered him a ride while his men walked. The general said, "Thanks, but we have been through thick and thin together. I think we'll stick together to the end." He walked. That is what it means to follow Jesus. It means to share in his promise,"Lo, I am with you always."

II

Second, we learn that to live is to learn to give.

Yes, that too. To follow Jesus is to be a person who has learned that the secret of living is found in giving. That is why the Dead Sea is dead. It receives, but has no way of giving. At one end of the Jordan River is the Sea of Galilee, a beautiful lake filled with fish and plant life. It receives and gives. At the other end of the Jordan River is the Dead Sea. But, it has no outlet. Nothing grows there because the Dead Sea cannot give.

Jesus knew and taught a great truth about life — that living is found in giving, and that death comes from grasping. And, so it was that he said, "Anyone who tries to save his life will lose it, but those who are willing to give their lives for my sake will find life."

This great truth is at the core of what it means to follow Jesus. And whether or not we follow Jesus affects everything we do, and everything that happens to us. It is not just "religion." It is choosing life over death.

Alfred Adler said, "All ills can be traced back to one thing — not understanding the meaning of the phrase, 'It is more blessed to give than receive.' "

Jimmy Carter spoke to a class at the theology school at Emory University not long ago. He referred to the hymn, "I Surrender All." He suggested we should sing, "I surrender ten percent of my life to God," — or twenty, or sometimes fifty — but never *all*.

A man learned he was going to die. His pastor went to see him. The man said, "I haven't done much for the church. If I give the church one million dollars, do you think that would get me into heaven?" The preacher said, "I don't know, but it's worth a try."

One morning during a revival meeting someone asked Dwight L. Moody how many conversions there had been the night before. He said, "Two and a half — two children, one adult who gave half his life."

When we follow Jesus we learn that to live — is to learn to give.

III

Third, we go where he leads us, and serve where he needs us. That is important too. To follow Jesus means to be going somewhere. We are following him toward something. We go where he leads us. We serve where he needs us.

He called the disciples to go with him, and they did. Simon

Peter went all the way to Rome. Thomas went all the way to India.

I know a man named John Stroud. He went all the way to Cuba. He was a missionary for years. He would go to a small town, announce a service in the square, preach to everyone in town, and organize a church. When Castro came to power he wanted John Stroud to work for the government. But John Stroud refused to quit preaching. One night an army sergeant came to his door, and said, "Come quick. Bring nothing with you." He took John Stroud and his family and put them on a plane to Miami. The next day the army came to arrest him. The sergeant had saved his life.

Where do you think God needs you? Maybe he needs you to simply be a person who is a Christian right where you are, in your job; or walking down the street; or singing in the choir; or teaching a children's class. If you are a young person, maybe God needs you to be a minister, or a missionary, or a doctor, or a teacher in some country where people need help — in Africa, or South America, places where the need is.

Would you go where he leads you, and serve where he needs you?

Leslie Newbigin was a student at Cambridge University in England, preparing to go into his father's business. He decided to spend part of a vacation working with the miners in South Wales who he said, had been rotting in misery for years. He had no success, and felt defeated. But one night, overwhelmed by defeat, he had a vison of the Cross. And he realized it was the only thing which could make sense out of life.

When he finished school he was asked to give one year of service to the British Student Christian Movement. That was all — just one year. But, he wound up in the ordained ministry. He became bishop of the Church of South India.

That happens when you hear, "Follow me, and I will make you become fishers of men."

Are you listening?

Chapter Three

Children's Object Lesson

"He Ain't Heavy"

Object: *A Pair of Crutches*

Good morning, boys and girls. I am glad to see you, and I'm glad you have come to church today.

This morning I want someone to tell us what this is. (Let them answer.) That's right. This is a pair of crutches. They have been adjusted to fit you. I want one of you to show us how to walk with crutches. (Let a volunteer demonstrate.) You did real well.

Now, I want to tell you a story I heard when I was about your age. A man was out in his yard one day, and he saw a boy coming up the street with another boy on his back. It was obvious the younger boy was crippled and unable to walk. When they came by the man he said, "Son, isn't he too heavy for you to be carrying on your back?" The boy replied, "He ain't heavy. He's my brother."

Some years ago someone took that story and made a popular song out of it. "He ain't heavy, he's my brother."

Our Scripture for today tells us that when Jesus saw the crowd he had compassion for them. This does not mean he had pity for them, or just felt sorry for them. He did something even better than that.

When Jesus looked at people who were sick, blind, alone, crippled, or afraid, he had compassion for them. This means he felt their pain in his heart. He took their pain upon himself, and he tried to help them.

And, boys and girls, Jesus wants to live in us in such a way that you and I would have this same kind of feeling. He wants us to be people who care about other people.

All of us know people who are sick, or have problems. Jesus wants us to love them. He wants to love them through us. This will mean that sometime we will take someone's burden on ourselves as we try to help them.

When we do that, we discover that this person, and this person's problem, is not heavy — because this person has become our brother or sister.

Jesus said one time, "My yoke is easy and my burden is light." When we help someone carry their load, we are letting Jesus love them through us.

Prayer: Let's pray together. **O God, help us to understand that many times people we know need your help, and that often it comes through us. In Jesus' name. Amen**

Thank you for being here with us today.

Chapter Three

The Master Has Come —
And Is Moved With Compassion

Matthew 9:35-38

There lived in India a well-known poet named Tagore. One morning his servant was late coming to work. Tagore became more angry by the minute as he waited for him to arrive. Finally, the servant came in and began his duties. Tagore had already decided to fire him. He said, "Stop what you are doing and get out. You are fired." The man kept sweeping and said, "My little girl died last night."

This incident points up one of the great needs in the world today — the need for compassion. Compassion has been defined as "sorrow for the sufferings of another, with the urge to help." But, we have cheapened the word. When we hear the word "compassion," we really think of pity — and we hear such nauseating phrases as "pity the fool." Pity is not worth a plug nickle. It was pity that caused one man praying in the temple to say, self-righteously, "I am thankful I'm not like that man over there."

No, we do not need any more pity. We have had enough of that. What the world longs for is compassion. George Buttrick, in *The Interpreter's Bible*, wrote that the word we translate as "compassion" is a much stronger word, meaning "the pain of love." That's it. Compassion is the pain of love.

The Master has come — and is moved with compassion.

After Jesus had announced the theme of his campaign, "The Kingdom of God is at hand," and had chosen twelve to be disciples, he set out on a preaching tour which carried him to small towns and villages.

Matthew tells us that Jesus taught in the synagogues, and preached the Gospel of the Kingdom. Not only that — he also healed those who had diseases and infirmities. As his fame began to spread, large groups of people came to hear and see him. They hung on every word. They longed for the healing touch.

Then, Matthew says, "When he saw the crowds, he had compassion for them, because they were harassed and helpless, like sheep without a shepherd." (Matthew 9:35-38) It was not pity Jesus had. He did not feel sorry for these people. He felt the pain of love.

We see this compassion of Jesus, this pain of love, in other places. On one occasion, a large crowd had come to hear him. After he had healed the sick he said to the disciples, "I have compassion on the crowd, because they have been with me now three days, and have nothing to eat; and I am unwilling to send them away hungry, lest they faint on the way." He took the loaves and the fish and fed the people.

On another occasion he went to the city of Nain. A man who had died was being carried out of the city, the only son of a widow. Luke wrote, "When the Lord saw her, he had compassion on her and said to her, 'Do not weep.'" Jesus restored the young man's life.

Then, once when Jesus was preaching in Galilee, a leper came up to him and said, "If you will, you can make me clean." Mark reports, "And Jesus, moved with compassion, put forth his hand, and touched him, and said to him, 'I will; be clean.'"

Everything Jesus did was rooted in this compassion — the pain of love. His words — the stern words, the comforting words, the healing words, the forgiving words, all had their root in the pain of love. His deeds of mercy stem from compassion. All the miracles of Jesus grew out of the pain of love. Never did Jesus do a miracle just for the sake of a miracle itself. Never did he try to impress an audience. No, instead you see Jesus being moved with compassion. He sees a pain, a hurt, a sorrow, a loss — and the pain of love causes him to reach out to touch, to lift, to help, to heal, to forgive, to transform, to encourage, to challenge.

The Master has come — and is moved with compassion. There are three things to remember about the compassion of Jesus.

I

We see the pain of love in incarnation.

It is the compassion God felt for his creation that caused Him to send Jesus Christ into the world. "Incarnation" is a fancy word which means God took on human flesh, and came into our experience. The pain of love was the motive force behind that incarnation. "God so loved the world that he gave his only son . . ."

God knew this was necessary because in spite of everything he had done for his children, still they were in trouble. He made them a covenant they had not kept. He gave them a law they had not obeyed. He sent them prophets they had not heeded. So now God would send them his Son to love them — to care for them, to touch them, to reveal himself to them, to win them, to convince them, to compel them.

Wherever Jesus went to help — and lift — and encourage — and heal — we see there the heart of God, the love of God, the compassion of God, the pain of God's love.

Love is often painful.

A young woman fell in love with a young man. They were going on a picnic. It was their first date. She was afraid he would find out how near-sighted she was. So, she went out to her uncle's farm, where they were to have the picnic, and stuck a pin in a tree. Later, as they were eating, she said, "Oh, look. Someone left a pin in that tree." She ran to retrieve it, and tripped over a cow.

Love is often painful.

But, the pain of God's love is good news for us because we are often like the people Jesus touched — the fallen, the blind, the deaf, the sinners, the lost, the least, the despised, the unloved. We are those people.

A little first-grader hurried into the classroom and said, "Teacher, two boys are fighting on the playground, and I think the one on the bottom wants you."

We sometimes feel life gets us down. God has sent Jesus Christ to rescue us — to show us the way, to help us, to meet us, to lead us.

An old rabbi told a story of a boy who ran away from home. He was one-hundred days' journey away. He sent his father a message that he wanted to come home, but he did not think he could make it. His father sent him a message back: "Go as far as you can, and I will come the rest of the way to meet you."

God has done that in the incarnation.

II

Second, we hear the pain of love in identification.

The pain of God's love, which sent Jesus into the world, is heard in his identification with us. For not only did Jesus come into the world, he became like us. He became one of us. He identified himself with us completely.

Saint Paul wrote in Philippians, "Though he was in the form of God, [he] did not count equality with God a thing to be grasped, but emptied himself, taking the form of a servant, being born in the likeness of men, and being found in human form he humbled himself and became obedient unto death, even death on a Cross."

Jesus Christ emptied himself. He changed places. He gave up the highest status and took the lowest, that of a servant. He became obedient unto death on the Cross. The pain of God's love, goes that far. It runs that deep. We hear it in Jesus identifying himself with us.

Martin Luther heard it. As a young man he wanted to be a lawyer. One day he was nearly struck by lightning — and decided to become a monk. But he lived a life of fear. Then he taught a course on the Psalms at Wittenberg University. As he was preparing a lecture, he came to Psalm 22 — "My God, my God, why hast thou forsaken me?" He was captivated by those words. He realized that by going to the Cross, Jesus, in his God-forsaken-ness, had taken upon himself the sin, the sorrow, the suffering, the fear, the frustration of Martin Luther and every person. And, for the first time Martin Luther found faith.

We hear the pain of God's love —

•when Jesus says, "I have come that you may have life, and have it abundantly;"

•when he says, "the Son of Man will be delivered into the hands of his enemies;"

•when he prays in the garden, "Let this cup pass from me . . ."

•when he screams from the Cross, "My God, my God, why hast thou forsaken me?"

It is a word we must hear — the word of his identification with us — for it is the Word of life. It is the word, the liberating word, we must hear to be set free.

He became like us that he could take our suffering upon himself. And, with his suffering, his defeat, he allows us to see there is a victory — a victory which comes only through defeat.

Before you get to Easter you have to go through the Cross. It was true for Jesus. It is true for us.

III

Third, we feel the pain of love in imitation.

This compassion God has for his creation — this pain of love we find in Jesus Christ, which he had for all sorts of people — is not only something to be seen and heard by us. We are called to feel this pain in our hearts. We are called to be people of compassion. Saint Paul said, "Therefore be imitators of God, as beloved children."

Much of our world today is unfeeling, uncaring, unconcerned. Two hunters paid a high price for a bird-dog. They took him out for a field test. After an hour one said, "This dog is no good. We might as well put him to sleep." The other said, "Let's throw him up in the air one more time. If he doesn't fly this time, we'll shoot him." Many people have such an attitude toward persons. We elevate things to the level of persons. We lower persons to the level of things.

If we call ourselves Christians, if God has laid his hand on us, if Jesus has claimed our allegiance, then we simply cannot be like the rest of the world. God has called us to care, to have compassion, to feel the pain of love in our hearts. God has called us to share the love we have received.

E. Stanley Jones told about a man who went to his back door and found a dog with a hurt leg. He took the dog in, bandaged the leg, and fed him for several days. When the dog was well again, he let him out, and the dog ran off. The man was disappointed that the dog had no appreciation for what he had done. But, the next day he looked out and there was the dog again — and this time he had with him another dog with a hurt leg. That is what we are called to do — bring someone else, share with someone what we have received, feel the pain of love in our hearts.

But, even as we do this there is the danger that our compassion takes on the form of mere pity.

There is a story of the Dutch Governor General of Java. He was complaining because the people wanted the Dutch to leave. He told a companion, "Look what we have done for them." He listed the schools, hospitals, elimination of disease, honest government, peace, roads, railroads, industry. He said, "Yet, they want us to go. Can you tell me why they want us to go?" The man said, "I'm afraid it is because you've never had the right look in the eye when you spoke to them." Perhaps it was the look of pity — or disdain, or revulsion, but, it was not the look of compassion.

Jesus had the look of compassion.

Matthew said, "When he saw the crowds, he had compassion for them." Then, Jesus said to his disciples, "The harvest is plentiful, but the laborers are few; pray therefore the Lord of the harvest to send out the laborers into his harvest." Jesus Christ is calling us to be that — the people of compassion, people who feel the pain of love in our hearts.

For many years Anton Lang played the part of Christ in the passion play at Oberammergau. One day a friend was looking around the set. He saw the Cross, and tried to pick it up. He thought it would have been a fake cross. But, it was made of real timbers. He said, "Why is it so heavy? How do you carry that cross?" Lang answered, "If I did not feel the weight of his cross, I could not play his part."

Compassion is something we cannot fake. No play-acting will do, for the stakes are high, the times are dangerous, and God needs a people to be like him.

Chapter Four

Children's Object Lesson

"Building a Church"

Object: *A Brick*

Boys and girls, it is good to see you in church today. I am glad you are here. Today I want to show you something. Who can tell us what this is? (Let them answer.) Right. It is a brick.

Who can tell us what we use bricks for? We use bricks to build things don't we? I know you have seen many brick buildings. [Our church is made of bricks.]

I used to be the pastor of a church which was made out of rocks. They were large stones from a farm just outside of town. Many buildings today are made of brick, though.

Did you know there are many places in the Bible where building something out of stone is mentioned?

In one place, at the close of the Sermon on the Mount, Jesus said if we live by his words we will be like a man who built his life on the rock. When the storms came his house stood firm. But, if we do not build our lives on his words we are like a man who built his life on sand. When the storms came, his house fell in.

Then, in another place which is in our Scripture today, Jesus told Simon Peter he would build his church on the rock of Simon's faith. In fact, the name Peter means "The Rock." Simon had faith in Jesus and believed Jesus was the Christ. So, Jesus said to him, "Simon, you are a rock, and on the rock of your faith I will build my church." The church is always built upon faith in Jesus Christ.

There is another passage in the Bible which says that Jesus is the chief cornerstone of the church. That means the church is built on him.

How many of you know the hymn, "Rock of Ages"? Jesus Christ is the solid rock upon which we build the church, and also our own lives. So, I want you to remember this today. We all need a strong foundation upon which we can build our lives, and also our church. There is only one true foundation — Jesus Christ, God's Son. We can bet our lives on him.

Prayer: Let us bow our heads now for prayer. *O God, we thank you for your son Jesus Christ. Help us to build our lives on him, and we ask it in his name. Amen*

I want to thank you for being here in church today.

Chapter Four

The Master Has Come —
To Build His Church

Matthew 16:13-20

I remember being on a trip in Tennessee and coming to a crossroads. One road went to Copperhill; the other went to Norris Dam. There at the crossroads was a little white frame church. The church stands at every crossroad.

The Christian Church was no accident. It did not just happen. It was not merely a sociological phenomenon, a quirk of history. It was not founded upon a lie, an idea, a philosophy, hope, a dream, a delusion. It was planned, intended, constructed, trained, sent, commissioned, blessed, empowered, and directed.

The Master has come — to build his church.

One day Jesus stood at the crossroads. He and the twelve were up in the district of Caesarea Philippi. It was a place filled with much symbolism.

The town was named for two Roman rulers — Caesar Augustus and Philip. There was a Greek temple there, built in honor of the Greek god Pan. It was located near the headwaters of the Jordan River. So, the place was alive with the symbolism of Rome, Athens, and Jerusalem.

It was somewhere out in the country that Jesus must have stood on a little hill, and looked far off down south toward Jerusalem. As he stood there looking, the wind blew his hair across his face. He brushed it back, and said to the twelve: "Who do men say the son of man is?" They answered, "Some say John the Baptizer, Elijah, Jeremiah, or one of the prophets."

Then Jesus turned toward them, and gave them that look only he possessed, and said, "But, who do *you* say I am?" As soon as the words fell across his lips Simon answered abruptly,

"You are the Christ, the son of the living God." Jesus replied, "Blessed are you, Simon Bar-Jona! For flesh and blood has not revealed this to you, but my Father who is in heaven. And I tell you, you are Peter, and on this rock I will build my church, and the powers of death shall not prevail against it. I will give you the keys to the kingdom of heaven."

Then Jesus and the twelve took that road which led them down toward Jerusalem. Matthew tells us, "From that time Jesus began to show his disciples that he must go to Jerusalem, and suffer many things."

The Master has come — to build his church.

We are in the church today because the Master has come — because he has put the church here, and has called us to be in it. Carlyle Marney said, "The reaction to who Jesus is puts us in church always." The *Master* has come — and we are the church. Would you remember this about the church the Master has come to build?

I

The church has a message.

That is the first thing to remember about the church the Master has come to build: it has a message.

The church is built upon the affirmation that Jesus is Christ. "You are the Christ, the son of the living God." This is the message of the church. We must never forget this. The message is the motive. We have no other reason for being except that Jesus is Christ.

If Jesus is not Christ, then let's all go home and quit fooling ourselves, for we have nothing to offer the world. If Jesus is not Christ, then we are no more than a civic club which meets on Sunday. The church does not even make a good civic club. The message about who Jesus is has created the church. He is Christ. We must remember this always.

Sometimes people say the church is old-fashioned, has old-fashioned beliefs, and is stubborn about holding onto them. The church had better hold onto them. That is all it has. We need to relate this message to the age in which we live, but we dare not *become* the age in which we live. Dean William R. Inge said when the church marries the spirit of the age she will become a widow in the next generation. We must hold onto our old message or become something less than church.

A young man went into a beautiful new library. He stood there on the first floor, and looked around at glass-covered display cases, stamp collections, marble statues, pictures, various announcements about classes and activities offered, magazine racks — and then said with a bewildered look, "Where do they keep the books?" He thought a library was a place for books.

A grand post office was built in a certain town. It cost several million dollars. But when it was opened and dedicated, it was discovered that the architect had left out one thing. There was no place to mail a letter. A post office is for letters.

Not long ago I rode by a church which had something on its bulletin board out front which greatly bothered me. There was no sermon title, worship invitiation, or catchy sentence. Instead, there were these words: "Karate Classes Every Tuesday." I thought to myself (after I got the car back on the road), "What does that have to do with church? What good would that do a person coming by here looking for hope, help, light, love?" Breaking someone's face with the side of your hand has absolutely nothing to do with the message of the church. A church has a message about Christ or it is not a church.

Do you know why the message is so important? Because it is the only answer for the problems we face, and the problems of the world.

Two hunters got lost. One remembered reading that if you ever get lost while hunting you should shoot three times in the air. They tried it. No help came. They tried it again. No help. One asked, "What do we do now?" The other said, "I don't know. I'm all out of arrows." Without the message about Jesus being Christ we are like lost hunters shooting arrows in the air. No one hears them, nor our cries for help. No one even cares.

But Jesus the Christ cares. God cares. Help is on the way. Help has come. That is the church's message. Jesus is Christ.

II

The church has a Master.
That is the second thing we need to know about this church the Master came to build. He is the Master of the church. The church has a Master — a Lord, a leader, a head, a foundation — none other than Jesus who is Christ. Jesus said to the disciples that he would build his church on the affirmation of the rock-man, Simon Peter, and that "the powers of death will not prevail against it."

The church has a Master — someone who builds, inspires, and leads the church, someone whom the church worships, serves, and imitates. Jesus the Christ is Master of his church. We must remember not only the *message*, but also the *Master*. If we do not remember who the Master is, the message gets lost. We forget it, warp it, twist it, or make it into some old or new heresy.

When Christians take their eyes off the Master, they become something other than Christian — and their church becomes something other than a church. When we take our eyes off the Master we begin thinking the church is ours instead of his. We seek our will instead of God's will.

When I was six years old, my father was sent to be the pastor of a church in south Georgia. The church badly needed an educational building. Everyone in the church wanted to build it except for three men. They opposed it, and said the church did not need it. They each said, "Over my dead body." They should not have said that. I am glad to report that after a year the building was on the ground. I am sorry to report that the three men were under the ground. It was built almost literally over their dead bodies.

Don't bet against God. Jesus said not even the powers of death would defeat his church.

At the theology school at Emory University named for Bishop Warren A. Candler, there is a statue of the bishop. When I was a student I would often stop and look at it, and think about the words on the inscription, "A master among men whose master was Christ."

The church has a Master.

III

The church has a mission.

That is the third thing to remember. A church with a message and a Master always has a mission. The mission is to spread the message about the Master. That means it is our mission to tell the world about Jesus who is Christ. Jesus said, "I will give you the keys to the kingdom." He entrusted the disciples with a mission.

At first glance you might think that is a narrow definition of the task at hand. But, this does not mean we simply announce "Jesus is Christ," and that is it. It does not mean hands off everything else, don't meddle — don't get into anything controversial, don't dabble in politics, economics, war and peace.

It does *not* mean we just say, "Jesus is Christ" and sit around with smiles on our faces while the whole world goes to hell. If Jesus is Christ then everything in the world comes under his sovereign rule. Every issue is seen clearly only in the light of his ethic. Every problem finds its solution only in the depth of his understanding. Every sorrow finds a comfort only in the width of his mercy. That is why the mission of the church is so vitally important.

A man was charged with being drunk and setting a bed on fire. When he went before the judge he said, "Your honor, I am guilty of being drunk, but that bed was on fire when I got in it."

The world was already in trouble when the church got in it, and it still is. Without the church's mission — its message about the Master — the world does not stand a chance, for we are bound and determined to destroy ourselves and each other.

Jesus Christ always has been, is today, and always will be the hope of the world. Truly, Jesus is the world's *only* hope. If you do not believe that, then you are living in a dream world, a world which will not long endure. That is why the church has a mission. That *is* the mission. That is why it is vital that we make some choices about who will have our allegience, and what will be our priorities. That is why the Master still calls us today to be Christian, to be discipled, to be church.

In the early days of the church there were some Roman soldiers who had become Christians. They were going to be put to death because of their faith. There were fifty of them. They were marched out onto a frozen lake — told to remove their clothing — and were left there to freeze to death.

As they stood on the ice they were singing together, "Fifty soldiers of the Cross, and all prepared to die." But, then the song changed to "Forty-nine soldiers of the Cross, and all prepared to die." Those on the bank saw one of them coming toward land, putting his clothes back on.

Then, one of the Roman officers stepped out onto the ice, and began walking toward the Christians. He took off his clothing, and disappeared in the blowing snow. And, the song changed again: "Fifty soldiers of the Cross, and all prepared to die."

Jesus the Christ is calling us to be "rock people" — people upon whose faith he can build his church.

Would you be a rock person for Jesus?

Chapter Five

Children's Object Lesson

"A Call From God"

Object: *A Telephone*

Hello, boys and girls. Isn't it good to be here in church together today? I am glad you are here.

Now, I know all of you know what this is. It is a telephone, and I will bet all of you talk on the phone. It is easy to talk on the phone isn't it? All you do is dial the number and talk.

Do any of you have a grandmother who lives far away? How often do you talk on the phone to her? (Let them tell you.) Not only do we like to call other people, but we like for them to call us. It is nice to hear the phone ring and have someone say, "The phone is for you." Then we know there is someone there who wants to talk with us.

Did you know that God is calling you? In our Scripture lesson today, we will read how Jesus went to see some good friends of his when one of them died. The man who died was Lazarus. His sisters were Mary and Martha. And, one of the verses in this story is one of my favorites: "The Master has come and is calling for you." And, I want to tell you today that this is still true for us, even now. The Master is still calling for you. Oh, he does not call us on the phone. But, he does call us to believe in him, to follow him, to serve him. He calls us in many different ways. Sometimes we feel in our hearts that God is speaking to us. We hear God's call as we pray, and we know he is answering us. At other times God calls us as we read the Bible, study in Sunday church school, worship in church. Or, maybe God calls us as we see some problem or hurt that we can do someting about.

God calls us in many ways and he is calling each one of us to be a child of God, and to serve him. So, be sure to keep on listening, because God is calling you.

Prayer: Would you bow your heads for prayer now? *Dear God, help us to be listening, and to answer the call you send us. In Jesus' name we pray. Amen*

Thanks for coming today, and sharing this time with us.

The Master Has Come —
And Is Calling For You

John 11:17-29

When I was a student in seminary we served a country circuit which had four churches. One of them was Allen-Lee Memorial, named in part after Young John Allen. It was located in the community of Lone Oak, Georgia.

When Young John Allen was fifteen he attended a revival at the Methodist church in Lone Oak. During the service he became so deeply convicted of the need of salvation that he jumped out of a window of the church and ran off in the woods to hide. But, he returned to the church, and gave his life to Christ. Eight years later, in 1859, he sailed to China as the first Methodist missionary in that vast empire.

I have read letters he wrote back home to relatives. I have seen the Bible he and his family read each night. And, I have thought often of how God used the life of a country boy from Georgia to open the way for the Gospel in China. His great work there still bears fruit even today.

I

The Master has come — and is calling for you.

The story of Jesus coming to Bethany at the death of Lazarus is filled with beauty and despair, drama and pathos, joy and sorrow. It is a human story which touches our human hearts. It sweeps us up in this suffering we see — and we know we have been there. In a very real sense it is the story of all of us.

The Master has come, — and is calling for you.

Word came to Jesus that his good friend Lazarus was ill.

Jesus was close to this family. He, no doubt, had spent much time with them. Jesus loved Martha, Mary, and Lazarus. It seems strange that Jesus did not leave immediately for Bethany to be with them in this time of illness. John tells us plainly that Jesus decided to wait until Lazarus died before going to see them. He said to the twelve, "Lazarus is dead; and for your sake I am glad that I was not there, so that you may believe. But let us go to him."

By the time they arrived Lazarus had been dead several days. When Martha heard Jesus was on the way, she went out to meet him. She said to Jesus, "Lord, if you had been here, my brother would not have died."

Perhaps those words contained not only sorrow, but also disappointment — and maybe anger at Jesus for not being there. But, she adds, "And, even now I know that whatever you ask of God, God will give you." Those are words of hope.

Then, in that poignant moment, Jesus said, "Your brother will rise again." Martha answered, "I know that he will rise again in the resurrection at the last day." And Jesus said, "I am the resurrection and the life; he who believes in me, though he die, yet shall he live, and whoever lives and believes in me shall never die. Do you believe this?" Martha said to Jesus, "Yes, Lord; I believe that you are the Christ, the son of God, he who is coming into the world." Martha then went to find her sister Mary, and said to her, "*The Master has come* and is calling for you."

You remember the rest of the story. When Mary came to where Jesus was, she fell at his feet. John tells us Jesus "was deeply moved in spirit." Then, we come to the shortest verse in the Bible, "Jesus wept."

When I was in about the third grade in Sunday church school, we had to recite Bible verses. I would always come in with something like, "The Lord is my shepherd . . ." I remember two boys who had the same verses every Sunday. One would say, "God is love." The other would say, "Jesus wept."

Jesus wept. The words tell us much about the humanity of Jesus. He went on to the tomb, and called Lazarus out of the tomb, "Lazarus, come out." And, he did. Then Jesus told the people to unwrap Lazarus, "Unbind him, and set him free." (John 11:17-29)

In this story, as with so much in the Gospel of John, there is the *outward* truth and the *inner* truth — the behind-the-scenes meaning of the event.

There is much here we could look at. But the great truth I want us to look at is this: *"The Master has come, and is calling for you,"* still today.

I

The Master comes to wherever we are.

Jesus went to Bethany to be with his friends in this time of sorrow — to share with them, to be a part of it, and to do something about it.

Jesus always sought people out. The New Testament affirms that he was God's son who came to the world, that in him God sought out all creation. This is the meaning of his life, death, and resurrection. The Master comes to us wherever we are.

The Bible affirms this truth from one end to the other. God looked for Adam in the garden and found him. He looked for Paul on the road to Damascus and found him. In between those two it is the same story all the way through.

There is another truth here too, and that is the fact that we are not all in the same place, and do not have to be in order to be found by God. We do not have to be in the same place socially, culturally, economically, intellectually, theologically. I read about a lady in a church choir who was so exuberant that she always sang ahead of everyone else. One night the choir was rehearsing the Twenty-Third Psalm. The choir director said, "Will the lady who gets to the still waters first please wait there for the rest of us." We are not all in the same place, but wherever we are, God seeks us out. He pursues us.

We often speak of someone finding God — or finding Christ — or finding truth, as though God or Christ or the truth had been lost! The real truth is that God has already found us, has sought us out, has pursued us. Years ago Francis Thompson, an unknown poet, published a poem he called "The Hound of Heaven."

> *I fled Him down the nights and down the days;*
> *I fled Him down the arches of the years;*
> *I fled Him down the labyrinthine ways*
> *Of my own mind; and in the mist of tears*
> *I hid from Him, and under running laughter . . .*
> *From those strong feet that followed, followed after.*

That poem was translated into over sixty languages. It had such a wide appeal because it told a great truth about God coming to find us.

In the harbor at Genoa, Italy, visible beneath the surface of the water, is a large statue of Christ. It was placed there in memory of those who died at sea in war. It is called the "Christ of the Deep." He comes to the depths of life, wherever we are.

II

The Master calls us whoever we are. That is the second thing to remember.

When Jesus arrived at Bethany he met Martha. Then, Martha went back to their home, and said to Mary, "*The Master has come,* and is calling for you."

Jesus went to the tomb of Lazarus, and called him out of the tomb, away from death to new life. Not only does he come to us; he also *calls* us, whoever we are. He speaks the words of life to us.

Jesus called the most unlikely people to be disciples — fishermen, tax collectors, people in different political parties, of various dispositions, talents, interests. He still calls us today, whoever we are. It does not matter who we are. He is able to take us as we are, and make us into those people he wants us to become — the people God designed us to be, the children of God. We are all eligible for that, no matter how we feel, live, or look.

Early one morning a lady heard the garbage man outside

her door. She ran to the door, and said, "Am I too late for the garbage?" He took one look at her and said, "No lady. Hop right in." Whoever we are, the Master calls us.

John wrote at the beginning of his Gospel: "To all who received him, who believed in his name, he gave power to become children of God." We are called to become the children of God.

There are many things calling us these days. A man was awakened by the phone at two o'clock in the morning. The voice at the other end said, "Your dog is barking, and he is keeping me awake." The sleepy neighbor was not alert enough to make an intelligent reply. The next morning at two o'clock he called his neighbor and said, "I don't even *have* a dog."

There are many things calling us — many demands being made upon our living. There are many diversions which interrupt life, calling us away from our best selves. There is one call we cannot escape. God has a claim on our living.

John Baillie wrote, "My earliest memories have a definitely religious atmosphere. I cannot recall a time when I did not feel in some dim way that I was not my own to do with as I pleased, but was claimed by a higher power which had authority over me."

God has a claim on our living — whoever we are.

III

The Master can use us whatever we are. That is the third thing to remember.

When Jesus called Lazarus out of the tomb he said to those standing nearby, "Unbind him, and set him free." Jesus used those people to remove the cloth bindings from Lazarus — to unwrap and unbind him. It took no particular talent or ability to do it — just the willingness to help. The Master can use us, whatever we are, whatever we can do, whether or not we think we can even do anything. He can use us to set someone free. He can use us to lift someone's hope. He can use us to fill someone's stomach. He can use us to show someone the way.

You and I are the only version of God, of Christ, of the church, of the Bible — we are the only love, the only mercy, the only kindness some person will ever see. "Unbind him, and set him free."

As a young man, Albert Schweitzer was a preacher, teacher, theologian, and a masterful musician. He was known throughout Europe. But, he had the feeling something was missing. One day he read about some people in Africa who were receiving no medical attention at all. He put the newspaper down and said, "At last I have found a job that is big enough." He enrolled in medical school, spent years in training, and then went to Africa as a medical missionary. He opened his little hospital in the jungle, and spent the rest of his life serving there. Once while he was on furlough he was speaking to a group of students in Europe. He said, "The only ones among you who will be happy are those of you who will have sought and found a way to serve."

He knew this was true, for as a young theologian he had written a book, *The Quest of the Historical Jesus*, in which he said in the closing pages,

> *He comes to us as One unknown, without a name, as of old, by the lakeside, He came to those men who knew Him not. He speaks to us the same word: "Follow thou me!" and sets us to the tasks which He has to fulfil for our time. He commands. And to those who obey Him whether they be wise or simple, He will reveal Himself in the toils, the conflicts, the sufferings which they shall pass through in His fellowship, and, as an ineffable mystery, they shall learn in their own experience who He is.*

The Master has come, and is calling for you — wherever you are, whoever you are, whatever you are.

Chapter Six

_____

Children's Object Lesson

"Who's the Boss?"

Object: *A Crown*

Boys and girls, I am glad to see you in church this morning.

Today I want to show you a crown. Can all of you see this? There are many different kinds of crowns. They are not all alike. But, all of them tell us that the person wearing them are kings or queens, princes or princesses.

Who can tell us what today is? (Let them answer.) That's right. Today is Palm Sunday. This is the day when we remember how Jesus went into the city of Jerusalem. All of the people lined the street, and welcomed Jesus as the king of the Jews. They shouted "Hosanna! Blessed is he who comes in the name of the Lord." They welcomed Jesus as a king, but many of those people did not really mean what they were saying.

I want to ask you a question today. How many of you watch the T.V. program, "Who's The Boss?" All of you watch it? Do you watch it every week? I want to confess to you that I really do not watch that program. But, I do like the title of it, "Who's The Boss?" Do you know why I like that title so much? Because this is one of life's really important questions: "Who's The Boss?" That is a question every person has to answer. Every person has to decide who will be the boss of his or her life.

You are already faced with that question even now at your age. Who *is* the boss? And, I want to tell you that you will be facing this question the rest of your life.

It is simply a matter of how you are going to live. How are you going to decide how to live, what to do with your life, and how to make your decisions?

I want to tell you there is only one person in the world who is worth giving your life to. That person is Jesus Christ. If you will make him your boss, he will always treat you right, and he will always help you.

Will you allow Jesus to come into your heart and be your boss? I hope you will.

Prayer: Let us bow our heads for our prayer now. *Lord, we open our hearts to you. Come into our hearts, and be the one who is in charge of our lives. In your name we pray. Amen*

I want to thank you for being here on Palm Sunday.

Chapter Six

The Master Has Come —
To Face Jerusalem

Mark 11:1-10

During the last part of the nineteenth century there was a well-known preacher in England named Thomas Cook. He was going to preach in a certain town over a weekend. The people who were to keep him in their home talked about him so much their maid got sick of hearing about him. She went to the butcher shop on Saturday and mentioned all the fuss to the butcher. She said, "You would think Jesus Christ was coming."

But, the preacher captivated her too with his messages about the Master, and on Sunday night she dedicated her life to Jesus Christ. On Tuesday she went back to the shop and the butcher asked, "Did Jesus Christ come?" The girl said, "Yes, he did."

The Master has come — to face Jerusalem.

Palm Sunday — and the world is armed to the teeth, ready to blow itself up with the slightest touch of one finger on one sensitive button.

Palm Sunday — and there are fights between whites and blacks in two Georgia towns; the Ku Klux Klan raises its ugly head every now and then; and the South African government still gets away with murder.

Palm Sunday — and the Israeli army murdered some CBS newsmen; the Russian army murdered an American army officer; and both governments say, "We are not to blame."

Palm Sunday — and an irresponsible high school principal threw his student body into a panic when he announced over the PA system that we are being attacked by the Russians (just to see how they would react).

Palm Sunday — and Jesus is going into Jerusalem again, to face its hatred, skepticism, and deceit.

Palm Sunday — and Jesus is going to the Cross, to die for a world we would give up on were it not for him, and what he did.

No, the world has not changed much since that day when Jesus entered the city of Jerusalem. All our old hatreds, fears, and prejudices are still with us. We have simply dressed them up — and this world — in modern clothing.

The old Jews had always welcomed their kings to Jerusalem with shouts of "Hosanna! Blessed is he who comes in the name of the Lord!" And, they would wave palm branches as the king would ride by on a donkey.

And so they welcomed Jesus to the city. Someone had said he would be a new king, or something like that. Someone thought he heard someone else call him "the king of the Jews." Everyone was there. All good Jews who were able had made this trip to the holy city for Passover week. Many of these visitors from out of town had been captivated by Jesus back up there in Galilee. They had heard him, and had witnessed the things he did. So, now here he is, on what would become, not a day of glory but merely the prelude to a day of infamy. (Mark 11:1-10)

The Master has come — to face Jerusalem. And, his facing Jerusalem always brings about a time of decision, for that is what Palm Sunday means: a time of decision.

I

It was a time of decision for Jesus. It was a moment of truth for the Master.

Of course, he had really been making that decision all along. He made it the day he left the carpenter's shop. He made it in the wilderness during those forty days. He made it the day he and the twelve, up there in Galilee, took that branch of the highway at the fork in the road which led down toward Jerusalem.

As he paused out there on the edge of the city, he must have known there was still time to change his mind. He could still have waited a while longer, or have gone back. But no, he decided to go on — to keep riding toward the city. And, so he faced Jerusalem. He came to face his enemies. He knew they were there waiting, plotting, scheming against him. He did not run from a fight, nor did he back his way into it. They did not drag him screaming and yelling to the Cross.

A little boy came home with a black eye. His mother asked what had happened, and he told her he had a fight with Mike O'Reilly. She said, "I thought he was your best friend. What were you fighting about?" The boy told his mother he had called the Pope a bad name. She said, "A bad name! Didn't you know Mike was a Catholic?" He replied, "Sure, but I didn't know the Pope was."

Jesus was not like that little boy. He knew what he was getting into. He came to face his fears. He had fears — just as we do. Jesus was a man of courage. But, a person of courage is simply one who faces his fears courageously. Jesus faced his fears in the garden when his sweat was as great drops of blood, and he prayed, "Let this cup pass from me; nevertheless . . ." Nevertheless! He came to face the Cross. He knew it was there waiting. It had been there all along. He knew it was the culmination of who he was.

I went up in the church attic to find our old rugged cross. There it was in a corner, stuck back there with several years of dust and spider webs covering it. Made of the trunk of a small pine, with a stand of plywood, it was not too heavy — but, heavy enough. Getting those old windows off the stand was the problem, and then winding my way down the steps to the basement fellowship hall, and placing the cross on the stage for the children's program. It was not too heavy, but, heavy enough.

And, I said to someone I met on the steps, "If bearing the cross was this much trouble for Jesus, I don't know why he did it."

But we *do* know why he did it.

Centuries ago, on the island of Formosa, there was a ruler named Goho. He was a forward-thinking man who convinced the savage tribes under his rule to stop human sacrifices. Instead, they began using various animals for their sacrifices, animals which they believed would bring a good harvest. But one year the crops failed and the people became afraid. They thought the gods must be angry. Once again they demanded a human sacrifice. Goho tried to talk them out of it, but could not. So, finally he agreed. He told them to go to a certain place in the forest the next day, and they would find a man tied to a tree, wearing the red robe of sacrifice, and a red cloth over his head. That man would be the victim. The next day they did as he said — and they killed the man tied to the tree. Then, they discovered the man tied to the tree was Goho himself. From that day they never sacrificed another human being. By his death Goho did what his teaching could never do.

Jesus knew what he was doing and why. Palm Sunday was a time of decision for Jesus.

II

It was a time of decision for Jerusalem. It was a moment of truth for that city also. Jerusalem had to decide. Jerusalem was faced with a choice, no less than was Jesus himself. The burden was not only on the back of Jesus. It was squarely on the back of all Jerusalem.

A multitude gave him their cheers, but quickly turned the cheers into jeers. The people cried out, "Hosanna!" on Palm Sunday. But by Friday their anthem had changed to "Crucify!" Jesus washed the feet of the disciples on Thursday and Pilate washed his hands on Friday. A king was welcomed into the holy city and given a crown of thorns by an ungodly people. Jerusalem gave Jesus the key to the city — and changed the lock on its heart.

They rolled out a red carpet on Palm Sunday, dressed him in a purple robe on Friday morning, wrapped him in a white sheet on Friday afternoon, and placed him not on a throne, but in a borrowed tomb.

What a ghastly spectacle it was!

It was a time of decision for Jerusalem, and Jerusalem made its decision.

There was a town in south Georgia years ago which could not take the Gospel preached by God's man who had been sent there. They complained about his meddling in local affairs and not sticking to religion. They tarred and feathered that preacher, and rode him out of town on a rail. They made their decision. Go through there today and all that is left standing is the stump of a dead tree.

Palm Sunday was a time of decision for Jerusalem.

III

It is a time of decision for us today. It is still a moment of truth — but now, the moment faces us. Palm Sunday always confronts us with a decision. It is not just on the back of Jesus, and the back of Jerusalem. It is on our backs also.

We are Jerusalem. We are the people who stand and wait, who line the streets to watch the parade, who wave palm branches, and lift our voices in song , "Hosanna, loud hosanna!" *The Master has come* to face us, to confront us with a choice.

A game warden went fishing with one of his friends. They made their way out to the middle of the lake. The friend took out a stick of dynamite, lit it, and threw it in the water. When it exploded fish came up everywhere. The game warden said, "You can't do that." The man lit another stick of dynamite, handed it to the game warden and said, "Are you going to fish or sit there talking all day?" He fished.

Are we going to fish, cut bait, or what? "Then what shall I do with Jesus who is called Christ?" That is the question of Pilate. That is still the question. That is the question which faces us every day. You see, we are Jerusalem. We are the religious establishment — in the glow of stained glass windows, comfortable on padded pews, with mellow organ notes soothing our ears and drowning out the cries of the world. Jesus has come to face us, confront us, compel us, call us. Will we see him, hear him, obey him?

There is an old legend in the Talmud about a rabbi who talked with Elijah, and asked him when the Messiah would come. Elijah said, "Go ask him yourself." The rabbi asked where he was, and how he would know him. Elijah told him he could be found at the gates of the city, sitting among the poor and sick. So, the rabbi went to the gates and found him, and said, "Peace unto you, my brother and teacher." The Messiah replied, "Peace unto you, son of Levi." The rabbi then asked, "When is the Master coming?" And, the Messiah answered, "Today." The rabbi went back to Elijah and said, "He indeed has deceived me, for he said, 'Today I am coming' and he has not come." Then Elijah answered, "This is what he told you: 'Today if you would listen to my voice.' "

To all who say, "The Master has never come," or who say, "The Master will never come," or who say, "The Master is coming soon," I reply, "The Master has come — *today* — if you would listen to his voice."

What in the name of Almighty God will we do with Jesus who is the Christ? That question faces us today.

Chapter Seven

Children's Object Lesson

"Easter Means New Life"

Object: *A Cocoon*

Isn't this a great day to be together here in church? It is Easter Sunday, and that makes this a wonderful day.

Now, I want you to look at this. (Show them the cocoon.) Who knows what this is? Can anyone tell us? That is right. This is a cocoon. A butterfly lived in here for awhile. When he first went inside he was a caterpillar. He built this little nest to live in. Then when he came out he was a butterfly, and he flew away.

This is a good symbol of what Easter means. We talked last Sunday about Jesus coming to Jerusalem. You remember that on Friday Jesus died on the Cross. But then, on Sunday, Jesus was victorious over death. He came out of the tomb to live forever. In doing this Jesus has conquered death for all of us. God promises to give us eternal life through the victory of Jesus.

There are several things we do to remind us of what Easter means. We wear new clothes to help us think of new life. We have Easter eggs because they also remind us of the Resurrection, when Jesus came out of the tomb. We had our Sunrise Service today because the women went to the tomb, and found it was empty early that morning.

The new life Jesus gives us means more than going to heaven when we die. It means we can live a new life right now. And, we can let Jesus Christ be our risen Lord, the Lord of our lives.

There is a great old hymn we sing: "I serve a risen savior, he's in the world today." We *do* serve a risen savior. He *is* in the world today. And, he is here in our midst. He is with us now, to give us the gift of life. He will help us live the best life possible, both in this world and in the world to come.

And, he wants to be the Lord of your life.

Prayer: Would you pray with me? *Dear Lord, we are thankful for the good news of Easter. Be the Lord of our lives. For we pray in your name. Amen*

Have a good day, and thanks for sharing this time with me.

Chapter Seven

The Master Has Come —
To Be Lord of Life

Luke 24:1-11, 36-44

He was eight years old, and mentally retarded. His name was Stephen. I do not know much about him. I only read his story in another church's bulletin. But, I was touched by it. There were seven other children in his Sunday church school class. In the spring as Easter approached the children were asked to bring to Sunday church school those L'eggs panty hose containers, with some object inside which represented new life.

Not wanting to embarrass Stephen, and being afraid he had not understood, the teacher asked the children to place containers on the table to be opened one at a time. They opened the first and found a tiny flower, and one child said, "That's mine." They opened another, and found a rock. Another child said, "I brought that one." The child explained the rock had moss on it — a sign of life. They opened a third, and a butterfly flew out. Another child spoke up, "That was mine."

They opened the fourth and it was empty — and the teacher, knowing it must be Stephen's, reached for another. But, Stephen said, with halting speech, "Don't skip . . . mine." The teacher said, "But, it is empty."

And Stephen answered, "That's right. The tomb . . . was empty, and that is . . . new life for everyone."

That summer Stephen's condition became more serious, and he died. The children in his class attended his funeral. On his casket they placed eight L'eggs containers — all empty. That is what Easter means: an empty tomb.

The Master has come — to be Lord of life.

It was early that morning that the women made their way out toward the garden tomb to annoint the body of Jesus with spices. Slowly they walked those dark streets, took that little road out toward a grave in a garden. The first rays of light streaked across the sky. The sun peeped timidly over a hill, and reached its long arm down into the garden.

And, when they came to the tomb they discovered that great tomb door had been rolled back. What had happened here? They peered inside, then stepped in. There was no one there. The body of Jesus was gone. The tomb was empty. Their questions and thoughts were interrupted by those words, "Why seek ye the living among the dead?" What a question! Then, those heavenly voices said, "Remember how he told you, while he was still in Galilee, that the son of man must be delivered into the hands of sinful men, and be crucified, and on the third day rise."

"Yes, he did say that. We remember. But, we did not really believe it. It's really true!" They left the tomb, and hurried to find the disciples, who had been hiding out in the upper room since early Friday morning. They told the disciples the good news, but Luke, in his Gospel, records, "they did not believe them."

They must have spent most of that day debating what had happened. "Should we believe this? He *did* say this would happen. But, we saw him put to death. We know he was *dead*. John was there. So, where is he now, if the tomb is empty?"

Late that afternoon, two of their friends came in from Emmaus, and told of their experience with a stranger on the road — how he had come to their home and broken bread with them, and how they realized it was the Lord of Life.

Then, suddenly, Jesus came and stood in the midst of them. His unexpected appearance frightened them. But, Jesus said, "Why are you troubled, and why do questionings rise in your hearts? See my hands and feet, that it is I myself; handle me, and see; for a spirit has not flesh and bones as you see that I have. Have you anything to eat?" (Luke 24:1-11, 36-44)

He went on to show them how the words of the prophets had been fulfilled, and to tell them that they would be his witnesses when they received the power from on high.

The Master has come — to be Lord of life. Because of this, nothing has ever been the same since, nor will it ever be.

The Easter message is truly good news, Gospel for us. It is good news about the power of God, the power of good over evil, of life over death, of hope over despair, love over hate, good news about the Master's power.

Let me tell you some things about this one who has come to be Lord of life — and about his power.

I

The Lord of life has a power over death. Easter means that, first and foremost. There is a power over death. God is that power. It is expressed in Jesus Christ.

They put Jesus on a cross, and drove those nails with a loud thud, through his wrists, and they said to each other, "That's that. We have taken care of this problem. We don't have to worry any more about this 'king of the Jews.' " But, they didn't know that *wasn't* that.

They took him down from the Cross and sent him off to be laid in a tomb. They said, "We'll hear no more from him. He's dead and gone." But, they didn't know that, though he was dead, he *wasn't gone.*

Yogi Berra, that often-quoted baseball player, said, "It ain't over till it's over."

They did away with Jesus, and they said, "He's finished. His kingdom is over. This blasphemy is over." But they didn't know it *wasn't* over. It wasn't over until Easter morning. He has a power over death — and it's still not over.

God always has the last word. That is the good news of Easter. God has a power over death. We think death is the end, that with death everything is over. We dread it. We fear it. An angel came to see a man late in the night, and said, "I have some good news and some bad news." The man said, "Let me have the good news first." The angel then told him he had been selected to play in a golf tournament in heaven with Bobby

Jones, Bing Crosby, and Babe Ruth. The man asked, "What is the bad news?" The angel replied, "You tee off at eight o'clock tomorrow morning." Death is bad news for us.

Albert Camus said, "Because of death human existence has no meaning. All the crimes that men could commit are nothing in comparison with the fundamental crime which is death." Too many of us look at death in those terms: bad news. But Easter is the *good* news. Easter means the only thing that is over is death itself. Are you afraid of death? Have you lost a loved one? Then I have some good news for you. The Master has come — to be Lord of life. And the Lord of life has a power over death. "In my father's house are many rooms," he promised his disciples just the other night. Easter is the proof of it.

A little boy attended the funeral of his grandfather. He noticed there in the funeral home that everyone spoke in hushed tones. There was a somber atmosphere he did not understand. So, finally he said, "Why all this whispering? No one's asleep!" He captured what Easter means. The Lord of life has a power over death.

II

The Lord of life offers a power for living.

The message of Easter means more than something other-worldly. People who throw rocks at the church, and accuse Christians of simply wanting "pie in the sky, by and by" are misinformed. The Christian Gospel is not a fairy tale about streets of gold someday up yonder. The power of the Resurrection is a power for living.

The reality of the future life in God's Kingdom proves itself because it is a power for living in the present. Eternal life begins now. That means we do not have to be bound by fears and sorrows, toils and troubles, hardships and heartaches. There is a victory built into life. And, the Cross of Jesus Christ is the symbol of that victory. The Lord of life offers us a power for living.

He said to his disciples that afternoon, "Why do question-ings arise in your hearts?" We are troubled by many things, aren't we? Life has a way of getting the best of us. We let it get us down. There are times when some of us feel like giving up. The disciples felt that way that fateful Passover weekend. But, that was the last time they would ever be that low again. They would have their ups and downs later on. That weekend they learned, however, that they were serving a risen savior. That gave them a power for living. It gave them courage, hope, stamina. They discovered the abundant life of which they had heard Jesus speak. They could face anything.

Easter means that. The Lord of life offers us a power for living.

III

The Lord of life provides a power for witness. Easter offers this too, for the risen Lord empowered the disciples to become the church. He said, "You are witnesses of these things. And behold, I send the promise of my Father upon you; but stay in the city, until you are clothed with power from on high." The Resurrection of Jesus Christ provided a power for witness. It produced the church. And, the church is living proof of the resur-rection.

Something earth-shaking happened to these disciples which transformed their thinking and their living. They would not — could not — have gone out from Jerusalem to face the power of Rome were it not for the power of a risen Lord. Have you ever had anyone say to you, "How do you know the resurrec-tion is real? How can you prove it is true?" The answer is, "I do not have to prove anything. It proves itself. The existence of the church is proof enough — the church of a living Lord. Only a resurrection could have made it happen then, and could keep it going today."

The Christian church did not just happen. It had a super-natural beginning. The New Testament calls it "resurrection."

And, the living Lord, the Lord of life provides a power for witness today — the power to be Christian — the power to be church, the power to carry the Gospel to the world, the power to serve, to help, to lift, to encourage, to feed, to clothe, and to offer mercy — all in the name of God. Many people simply do not understand all this. But, we understand.

A missionary and his wife had spent forty years on the mission field. When they retired they sailed home. There was an army general on the ship. They had many conversations on the journey. The general could not understand these people, and why they had done all this hard work for no visible reward. When their ship reached the port, there was a great crowd there, waving and cheering. The army general was welcomed home as a hero. The missionaries were met by no one. But, as they wondered why, they seemed to hear a voice which said, "You're not home yet."

They smiled, for they knew at their home town train station all their friends would be there. They made the trip home, looking forward to seeing everyone. And, when the train pulled into the station they looked out the window. But there was no one there. The old man was overcome by disappointment. But, his wife put her hand on his, smiled, and said, "We're not home yet."

We are not home yet. *But, the Master has come* — to be Lord of life. And, that means everything will be all right.

About the Author

Thomas A. Pilgrim is a United Methodist Minister. He has served United Methodist congregations in North Georgia since 1966. He is the son of a minister, Dr. W. A. Pilgrim, Sr., and also has a son who is a minister, Reverend Thomas A. Pilgrim, Jr.

Reverend Pilgrim was educated at LaGrange College, and Candler School of Theology at Emory University. Reverend Pilgrim has written a weekly newspaper column, and is the author of *Faith For Today — And Tomorrow*. He has preached on the radio, in church revivals, and has spoken at various youth gatherings and civic clubs. He has been active on church boards and civic organizations. He and his wife Shirley have three children — Thomas A. Pilgrim, Jr., who is married to Donna Shelton Pilgrim; Andrea Sheri Pilgrim, who is employed by Cobb County Sheriff's Department; and, Christie Shannon, a junior high student.

Reverend Pilgrim is currently pastor at Maple Avenue United Methodist Church in Marietta, Georgia.